Jim Elliot

Mission to the Rainforest

Sue Shaw

OM Publishing
CARLISLE, UK.

ISBN 1-85078-104-4

**British Library Cataloguing in Publication
Data**

Shaw, Sue
    Jim Elliot : Mission to the Rainforest
    I. Title   II. Harley, Donald
    266.0092

    ISBN 1–85078–104–4

OM Publishing is an imprint of STL Ltd,
PO Box 300, Carlisle,
Cumbria CA3 0QS, UK

Designed and created by
Three's Company,
12 Flitcroft Street,
London WC2H 8DJ

Author: Sue Shaw
Illustrations by Donald Harley

Worldwide co-edition organised and
produced by
Angus Hudson Ltd,
Concorde House,
Grenville Place,
London NW7 3SA

Printed in Singapore.

The car refused to budge. Jim Elliot and his friends were stuck right in the middle of a level crossing, with a goods train heading straight towards them! Throwing open the car doors, they dived out. Seconds later the train ploughed into the car and demolished it.

This wasn't the first time Jim had escaped death. A few years before, he and a friend, Dick, were out shooting wild birds. Scrambling over a barbed-wire fence, Dick pulled the trigger on his gun accidentally. The bullet whistled through Jim's hair!

A few days after the train crash Jim wrote to his parents back home in Portland, Oregon: 'God kept me from harm. He must have some work that he wants me in somewhere.'

That work was to help Indian tribes people hear about God's love. The place was to be deep in the Amazonian rain forest of Ecuador, a country in South America. Here lived a small tribe of Indians called Aucas (pronounced *ow-kas*), who had never made friendly contact with the outside world.

Jim first heard about the Aucas when he was nineteen. In the summer of 1946 he joined hundreds of other Christian students on a language course at Oklahoma University.

They were all learning how to write down a language that had never been written before. It would be good training for Jim if he ever needed to translate the Bible into an unwritten language.

Who are the Aucas?

A missionary from Ecuador, who was asked to help Jim, told him about the Aucas. 'They make fire by rubbing sticks together on moss, they carry their babies in bark-cloth and sleep in hammocks. No outsider knows how to speak their language.'

Jim was fascinated. 'Have they ever met white men?' he asked.

'Yes,' the missionary replied, 'but they don't trust them. Years ago white men came to the forest with guns, hunting for rubber. They burned homes, attacked women and shot men. The Aucas only had spears to defend themselves with. For fifty years the hunters did as they pleased.

'Then oil was discovered. The oil companies built airstrips, houses and drilling rigs. The oilmen left gifts for the Aucas, to show they were friendly.'

'Did it work?' asked Jim excitedly.

'No. First the Aucas watched, then they attacked. Several men died, so the site was abandoned. No-one dared work there any more.'

Incredible, thought Jim. *These people have no idea that God loves them. Could they be the ones God sends me to?*

'This is for Ecuador'

After the language course, Jim spent ten days asking God about Ecuador. He read his Bible, praying; 'Please God, speak to me through your word. Help me to know what you want me to do.' Some words from the book of Exodus seemed to jump out of the page at him: 'I am sending an angel ahead of you to guard you along the way and bring you to the place I have prepared.'

Soon after, a letter arrived, with a twenty-dollar note inside. 'This is for Ecuador,' someone had written. They gave no name.

Another letter came, from a missionary friend in Africa who wanted Jim to know she was praying for him. Without realising it, her times of special prayer happened to be at the same time as Jim's.

Then Jim heard about the need for someone to work in
Ecuador among the Quichua *(keech-wa)* people, who lived in the
eastern forests, close to the Aucas. An English missionary, Dr
Wilfred Tidmarsh, had been working with the Quichuas for
twelve years, but his wife was ill and they needed to return to
Britain. Who would continue the work? Jim had no doubts. He
wrote: 'I dare not stay home while Quichuas die. The Quichuas
must be reached for Christ.'

His parents really wanted Jim to stay at home. They knew
American young people loved his lively talks about Jesus, and
he was in great demand as a speaker. But they weren't
surprised that he wanted to be a missionary. Jim's father had
spent much of his life travelling round America preaching, and
since he was six Jim had been telling people Jesus loved them!
Although he was a talented writer, speechmaker, building
designer and wrestler, Jim's greatest love was for preaching and
teaching the Bible, like his father.

The rest of the family understood too. His older brothers and his younger sister remembered their excitement as children when missionaries had stayed in their home. In fact, brother Bert was already in Peru working as a missionary doctor.

Jim applied for a passport and, while waiting to leave, teamed up with an old college friend, Ed McCully, to do handyman jobs. In their free time they studied the Bible together, made Christian radio programmes and wrote poetry.

Like Jim, Ed was excited about Christian work. But he was soon to marry and leave for Los Angeles to study medicine. Maybe they would all meet in Ecuador one day?

Jim in love
Jim also had thoughts about marriage. He had fallen in love with Betty Howard at the college where they had both been studying. They loved each other very much, but felt that the time wasn't right for them to marry. Betty was applying for jobs in different countries, and Jim didn't want to take a wife into the rain forest without knowing more about life there. So Jim prayed for another unmarried man to join him in Ecuador.

Pete Fleming from Washington had helped Jim at many Christian meetings. Like Jim, he loved the Bible, enjoyed travel and adventure, and was excited about work overseas. Pete, although engaged, wasn't planning to marry for a while. After hearing Dr Tidmarsh talk about his work, he was determined to go to Ecuador too.

Jim and Pete met in New York, then drove across America to Jim's home in Oregon, to prepare for their voyage to South America.

On New Year's Day 1952, Jim opened some letters that had arrived the day before. Each contained a cheque. Jim wrote in his diary: 'I discovered they totalled 315 dollars, my exact fare to Ecuador! Hallelujah!' It was a terrific way to start the New Year.

Sailing south

In February Jim and Pete set sail for Ecuador from San Pedro,
California. Jim had longed to go to sea as a boy, and now, at the
age of twenty-five, his childhood dream had come true.

They had great fun practising their Spanish on the other
passengers and the crew. And from the deck they spotted
turtles, flying fish - even a whale! On they sailed past Mexico,
Costa Rica, Panama and Colombia. After seventeen days at sea,
a small yacht drew alongside to take on passengers for Ecuador.
Pete and Jim loaded on their luggage. A four-hour sail brought
them to Guayaquil, a busy, modern port. It was baking hot.

The next day Dr Tidmarsh met them, and together they flew
to the capital, Quito *(key-toe)*. The city lay in a beautiful valley,
circled by high mountains and volcanoes. This was to be their
home for a few months while they learned more Spanish.

A runaway Auca

In Quito they learned more about the mysterious Aucas. A
young Auca woman called Dayuma *(dye-u-ma)* had run away
from her tribe to the outside world in fear of being killed.
Nearly all her family had been speared to death by her own
people. She told stories of Auca families fighting and killing one
another. They demanded revenge after each murder, so that
more and more people died. There were so many deaths that
the tribe had begun to grow smaller.

So Aucas kill each other too, thought Jim. *If we don't reach
them soon there'll be no-one left.* But before he could get close to
the Aucas, many other things had to happen.

There was a lot to learn. Besides Spanish classes, they had
lessons in simple medicine and tropical diseases. Then Betty
arrived in Quito, having accepted a job in Ecuador as a Bible
translator. Although they couldn't marry yet, they could at least
work in the same country.

Before Betty left the city, Jim showed her the sights. Together
they climbed mountains, watched a bullfight, explored the
cobble-stoned streets and studied Spanish.

In the rain forest

After five months' study, Jim and Pete squeezed on to a crowded bus for the long drive to the eastern forests, where the Quichuas lived. The bus shook and swayed along narrow rocky roads through mountains and earthquake zones, until they reached the edge of the rain forest. Rich green undergrowth and high thick forests spread for miles around; low, grey cloud filled the skies.

Dr Tidmarsh met them at Shell Mera, a small town that had once been home for oil diggers, and took them to an airstrip run by Christians. Travel in and out of the forest was easier and safer by plane, and saved many hours trekking through deep mud and water.

Soon they were flying over the jungle, heading for Shandia, where the Tidmarsh family had been working. There was no airstrip yet at Shandia, so they landed nearby and set out to walk the rest of the way.

They struggled over slippery rocks and roots, and waded knee-deep through thick squelchy mud. Towering trees blocked out the tropical sunlight. Brilliant-coloured fungi and delicate wild orchids grew everywhere. Noises of crickets and bats filled the air, and multi-coloured moths and butterflies fluttered overhead.

By the time they arrived at the doctor's thatched bamboo house the moon was rising. The house was built on stilts, so that fresh air could keep it cool, and protect it from the thousands of insects that lived in the damp earth.

Life with the Quichuas

Now Jim and Pete had come to live among the Quichuas, they had to learn their language. They also watched Dr Tidmarsh at work, taught in the school, and spent hours hacking away undergrowth so that they could build an airstrip and grow vegetables.

When Dr Tidmarsh left, Jim was thrilled to hear that his friend Ed McCully, with his new wife, Marilou, was planning to come to Shandia to work. So Jim set about building them a house.

Months passed. At times Jim wished things were going faster. *It's taking me ages to learn the Quichua language, and the building work is so slow,* he thought. *I wish Betty were here!*

A year had gone by since Jim had arrived in Ecuador. He decided to send a telegram to Betty: 'Meet me in Quito.' Betty took two days to reach Quito, first on horseback, then in a lorry. *I wonder why Jim wants to see me?* she thought. Jim was waiting for her with an engagement ring. Betty was thrilled!

Stormy days

Back in Shandia, Jim and Pete found the building work even slower, because the rainy season had arrived. Day after day rain poured down. Although it usually rains heavily for certain months each year, the Quichuas said this was the worst rainy season for thirty years. Part of the new airstrip was washed away. As the river rose higher, slices of river bank fell into the swirling water.

Jim and Pete tried to take down the houses to rebuild them

further from the river. But the rain beat down even harder. The river became a torrent, destroying everything in its path.

The two men could only watch as the water swept away the new homes, the clinic, the school and the kitchens – a whole year's work washed away in a few hours!

On hearing the news, Betty set off and arrived the next day. Betty understood how they felt. Only a few weeks before, all the Bible translation work she had done that year had been stolen, and there were no copies.

New plans

Eventually the rain eased, and they managed to rescue most of their belongings and pitch their tents. After Ed McCully arrived they made new plans. But they had to delay because Jim had an attack of malaria. He felt dizzy and had bad headaches. Unable to eat, he drank gallons of lemonade.

As soon as he felt stronger, Jim, Pete and Ed set off for three weeks to survey the forest and find other centres for their missionary work. Travelling on foot, or by dug-out canoe, they visited many Quichua homes.

The most promising place was Puyupungu, where the headman, Atanasio, asked them to start a school. They decided that Ed and Marilou should rebuild the centre at Shandia, and that Pete would stay and help them to learn Quichua. A husband and wife team were needed at Puyupungu. But who could go?

Jim immediately thought of Betty. 'How soon will you marry me?' he asked. Three weeks later they were married! After a holiday in Panama and Costa Rica, they flew back to Quito to prepare for setting up school.

At Shell Mera, on the edge of the rain forest, they stayed overnight with a pilot called Nate Saint and his wife, Marj. Nate loved to talk about the Auca Indians. 'I've flown my plane over Auca land many times,' Nate told Jim. 'I've not seen them yet, but I've met Quichuas who've been attacked by them.'

'Maybe one day we'll both fly out there and tell them about Jesus,' said Jim eagerly.

Nate drove Jim and Betty to the river, where they filled several canoes with their luggage - a steel trunk, a folding bed, a small oven and a tent. Punting the canoe down river, they headed towards their new base.

A new house

At Puyupungu, Atanasio gave them a warm welcome and gifts of fruit, eggs, smoked fish, drinking water and wood. Their new home was a thatched house. But it was far too small to stand up in and was crawling with cockroaches, so Jim pitched the tent instead.

Soon afterwards, Jim fell ill with a violent attack of jaundice, a tropical disease. He lay in bed for three weeks, hardly able to raise his head. The rain lashed down, seeping in under the tent, turning the dry earth into mud.

When the New Year came, he felt much better and began building a larger house and an airstrip. By April the airstrip was long enough for Nate to make a safe landing, and Jim and Betty were able to move into their new home.

They started to teach both the adults and children of Puyupungu to read and write in their own language. Together Jim and Betty talked to the Indian people about God's love. One day Atanasio said to Jim, 'I am very old. Perhaps too old to understand well. But it seems to me your words are true.' Jim and Betty were delighted.

Five families and the Aucas

Then news arrived from Shandia that Pete was flying back to America to marry his girl-friend, and that Ed and his wife wanted to leave Shandia to live nearer the Aucas. 'We'll have to move to Shandia and take charge there,' said Jim. 'Pete and his wife can continue our work here when they return.'

Meanwhile Nate and Marj stayed at Shell Mera, the base for the plane and for radio contact. Nearby another missionary couple, Roger Youderian and his wife, were working with the Jivaro *(he-va-ro)* Indians.

Soon there were five missionary families all living close to each other and to Auca territory. Had God brought them together so that Auca people could hear, for the first time, about God's love?

At Shandia, Jim spent many hours with a small number of Indian Christians, helping them study the Bible. At the same time, he began translating parts of the Bible into their own language. *The Bible is for everyone,* thought Jim. *With the Bible in their own language, the Indians can read it for themselves. I don't want them to think the Bible is only for foreigners or educated people.*

Soon several young Quichua men could understand the Bible and teach its truth. They began to preach, take Bible classes and lead meetings. Although it took time to get used to the idea, the Indians loved to see their own people in charge. One by one people started to ask questions about God and joined in the Bible classes. It was a very busy and happy time for Jim and Betty. It was great to see God at work!

The arrival of baby Valerie brought even more happiness. Jim loved being a dad. His parents arrived from America to see their new granddaughter and, soon afterwards, Jim's brother Bert and his wife visited from Peru.

There was always plenty to do. As well as teaching and translating, Jim made furniture and planted crops. The climate was ideal for growing fruit, vegetables and coffee. They ate home-grown corn, papaya, pineapple and avocado.

Jim also needed to be prepared for emergencies. He was often called out to people who had been bitten by poisonous snakes. *Don't leave home without your razor blade!* Jim often reminded himself. He needed it to cut the victim's skin, so he could suck out the poison.

Operation Auca

One day in September 1955, Jim heard the news he had long hoped for. Ed and Nate had finally spotted some Auca houses, when flying near Ed's house in Arajuno *(a-ra-hoo-no)*.

From that moment Jim couldn't stop thinking about the Aucas. He was bursting with excitement. *They're so near,* he thought, *and the work at Shandia is going so well. If only the same thing could happen with the Aucas.*

When news of their discovery reached Pete and Roger, the five men met to discuss how to contact the Aucas. They called their project 'Operation Auca'.

'Our first problem is how to learn the Auca language,' said Pete.

'Don't you remember when we first arrived in Quito?' said Jim. 'We heard about that Auca woman, Dayuma. She works for a Spanish landowner not far from here. Maybe she can help?'

Everyone agreed Jim should visit Dayuma, so he set off on a four-hour trek. He found she had forgotten most of the Auca language, except for a few basic words and phrases. Jim wrote them down carefully.

Gifts from the sky

The men decided to start sending the Aucas gifts. Nate invented a way of dropping gifts to the ground while still flying. A tin bucket, which could hold all kinds of things, was lowered from the plane on a long line. When it touched the ground, the bucket tipped up and out slid the gifts!

The first gift was a small metal kettle containing brightly coloured buttons and some salt. It landed close to an Auca house. The kettle was followed by a small knife. 'The plan is to drop different gifts every week, until the Aucas realise that

we're real friends,' explained Nate.

As the weeks went by, the Aucas began to look out for the plane. They stood waiting as the bucket spun down. On one trip Jim took a loudspeaker. As they neared the houses, Jim shouted out sentences in Auca that he had put together from what Dayuma had taught him. 'We like you. We are your friends! We like you!'

An Auca man shouted back while waving one of their gifts, a knife, over his head. They dropped a cooking pot holding a yellow shirt and beads. Arriving back home, Jim was so thrilled

he could hardly eat. On Jim's next flight they left a pair of trousers, a small axe, another knife and some plastic combs.

The Aucas began to tie their own gifts to the end of the line. They first sent up a headband of woven feathers, then combs made from reed. One week they sent a live red parrot in a small basket. They even included a banana, so the parrot enjoyed an in-flight meal!

Just before Christmas, the Aucas filled the bucket with cooked fish, meat and vegetables, peanuts, two squirrels, cooking pots and another parrot! It really looked as if they wanted to be friends. The men decided it was time to set up camp near the Auca village.

Palm Beach

Nate flew over the area to see if he could find a place to land. He rushed back to report. 'I've got some brilliant news. I've found some flat land on the edge of the river. The water has dropped, leaving lots of smooth, white sand. It'll make a perfect airstrip!'

'Fantastic!' said Jim. 'But we'll have to move fast. The rains are due in a month, and the river will flood again.' They agreed on a date to land – 3rd January 1956 – and gave their airstrip the code-name 'Palm Beach'. The plan was to build a tree house at Palm Beach and wait for the Aucas to visit. They agreed to take guns, but only to fire them to scare off any would-be attackers.

For a couple of days no-one appeared. It was very hot and sticky, with swarms of biting insects. Jim stood ankle-deep in the cool, clear water, with his word-list, shouting out friendly sayings in Auca. Suddenly a deep Auca voice boomed out from the trees. A young man, a woman aged about thirty and a young girl of about sixteen appeared on the other side.

Jim waded across to lead them back. Smiling, and using all the Auca words they knew, the Americans tried to show their visitors there was no need to be afraid.

George and Delilah

They nicknamed the man 'George'. He appeared to want a ride
in the plane, so Nate took him up over his village. George
seemed delighted. He waved and yelled to his people below.
They looked up in amazement!

Back on Palm Beach, George leapt out, clapping his hands.
Looking up to show the Aucas that they were talking to their
heavenly Father, the missionaries prayed aloud to God,
thanking him for all that had happened so far.

They spent some time showing the three Aucas things such
as balloons, rubber bands and a yo-yo. They served them
lemonade and hamburgers with mustard, and shot lots of
photographs and cine film.

The girl, whom they nicknamed 'Delilah', seemed impatient.
But the men couldn't work out what she was saying. Unknown
to them, she was Dayuma's sister, and thought Dayuma had
sent them. 'Where is Dayuma?' she kept asking. 'Where is my
big sister?'

As night fell, George and Delilah walked back into the forest. The older woman settled down on the beach. Early next morning Jim came down to start the fire and found that she had gone.

For the rest of the day they waited, but no-one came. Nate and Pete flew low over the village. The people ran about looking frightened. Nate threw down some shorts and a blanket. They flew over twice more. On the third trip George appeared, smiling. 'Perhaps everything's all right after all?' said Pete hopefully.

In fact the village people were arguing about what to do next. Some were angry that they didn't know more about Dayuma. Maybe the white men have killed her, they thought. The strangers must be up to no good. They forgot all about the gifts.

Missing

The Americans had arranged to send a message over the two-way radio at 4.30 that afternoon. Nate's wife, Marj, waited. Nothing. Not a sound. Was their transmitter damaged? Had they forgotten the time? The wives waited, unable to sleep.

Jim's wife, Betty, tossed and turned in bed. *What could have happened?* she wondered. *Why haven't we heard from them? Something must be wrong.*

Early next morning Marj asked another pilot, Johnny, to fly over Palm Beach. Johnny radioed back, 'No sign of the men. The plane has been ripped to pieces.'

Within hours the news had been broadcast round the world – 'FIVE MEN MISSING IN AUCA TERRITORY.' Johnny flew over again, and this time he saw a body floating in the river. A search-party was quickly organised.

They saw Ed's body first, on the beach. Then a helicopter crew spotted the other bodies – Jim, Nate, Pete and Roger – in the water. The Aucas must have ambushed them.

'We'll have to work fast,' ordered the search-party leader, 'in case there's another surprise attack. Some men stand guard, with guns ready to fire. The rest, start digging!' There was just

enough time to cover the grave and hold a burial service before
a huge downpour of rain forced them to leave quickly.

A few days later the wives flew over the burial spot. As the
small plane turned away, one of them said. 'That is the most
beautiful little cemetery in the world.'

Life out of death
Although their husbands had died, the wives all felt the love of
God very close to them, and wanted the work to go on. Each
one, in her different way, stayed in missionary work. Jim's wife,
Betty, remained at Shandia, teaching in the school, helping in
the clinic and translation work.

A year after the deaths, two Auca women walked out of the
forest, wanting to know if Dayuma was still alive. Dayuma met

them and agreed to go back with them to her village. Betty, full of forgiveness for the men who had killed her husband and friends, followed and lived with Dayuma's people for two years.

One by one the Aucas heard about God's love for them, just as Jim had prayed and hoped. Today many Aucas are Christians, including three of the men who killed the missionaries. Dayuma is now head of the church in her village, and the Aucas live at peace with each other and with the outside world.

Jim was twenty-nine years old when he died. As a student he once prayed: 'I seek not a long life but a full one, like you, Lord Jesus.' God heard that prayer, and many others too. Jim's life had been short. Yet we know that, as a result of his death and those of his friends, many Auca people became Christians and are telling others about Jesus today.